A

21st Century

Lazarus Experience

Bridget P. Dewees

A 21st Century Lazarus Experience

Unless otherwise indicated, all Scripture references are from the King James Version (KJV).

Cover Design: Bernard 'BJ' Brown/Southern Wave Media

ISBN 978-0-9828242-4-5 (Softcover)

Publishing Division
194 Avonshire Drive
Summerville, SC 29483
843-367-4496

This is dedicated to my "miracle man", James Dewees. In just 48 short hours, I was quickly reminded of the dedicated man God gave to me; why I fell in love with him, and what my life would be like without him. Could I do this alone? What would Justin do without his father? I clearly understand my role as his life partner as well as my contribution to the kingdom of God. James doesn't remember anything about the weekend that would change our lives forever; so, this also serves as a testimony of our love and path forward in Christ!

I love you Jay and Merry Christmas!
(2011)

In Loving Memory of
Lillian Rosetta Dewees

✠

Acknowledgments

A very special thank you to my Lord and Savior....

*...this is all about you **Jesus**!*

Special thanks to:

The entire Grant-Boone Wedding Party

♥

My assigned angels, nurses, EMS paramedics, doctors

♥

Apostle and Lady Simmons - New Bethel Sounds of Praise

♥

My immediate family, friends and church family

♥

Yakisha Simmons for encouraging me to pursue this vision

♥

A very special thank you to Tarsha Smalls for
letting God use you beyond your comfort zone.
You are an amazing Woman of God!

♥

The righteous, your prayers availed!

♥

My husband, James Dewees, the vessel God used for
this 21st Century Lazarus Experience.

Table of Contents

Foreword

Dec 2, 2011, changed my life forever. I do not remember what happened on that day, but I do know that God chose me for His glory. When I heard what happened, I was just in awe! 40 minutes...no pulse? No heartbeat? Most of all...God having prayer warriors in place to speak life and not death! This was overwhelmingly shocking! Wow! What a miracle! I know that if this had happened in a more subtle environment, it would be very hard to explain.

This doesn't happen in today's world without it being questioned or diagnostically challenged. Nevertheless, the fact that I had approximately 65 witnesses makes this story much more convincing. God wanted to be glorified and He wanted His people to know that He is still the same, just as He was in the days past. Yes...He is the same God that commanded Moses to stretch forth his rod over the Red Sea and the sea divided (Exodus 14:16). Yes...He is the same God that raised Lazarus from the grave after being dead 4 days (John 11). Yes...He is the same God that allowed Peter to walk on the water (Matthew 14:28). We can go on and on about these miracles of the past, but God wanted to give a wakeup call to the believers of today. I am an all-powerful God; the Alpha and Omega, the beginning and the end. Can God? Yes...He can and He proved it through me. How humbled I am that He decided to use me in this day and this hour.

As I begin to reflect on the lesson I've learned through this "Modern Day Lazarus Experience"...I would have to go back prior to the wedding rehearsal. I was taught that as believers, it is God's will that we cast all of our cares upon Him because He cares for us. He also knows how much we can bear (I Peter 5:7). This statement can sometimes be much easier said than done...at least for me. During the week prior to the wedding rehearsal, I picked up a burden that I knew I couldn't bear alone, but I felt that it was my responsibility to fix it. As a matter of fact...now that I remember, I also prayed and asked God to fix it. However, I still worried about it deeply. How often does this happen where we say we trust God and believe that He will take care of the matter; yet, we still have doubt in our hearts and minds. That's why I believe that God allowed this experience to happen. It wasn't just for me. He also wanted to give this assurance to all those who witnessed this experience as well. My God did fix the issue, but He definitely gave me a new revelation. If I can't fix it, then I won't worry about it. Also, if I placed it in His hands to fix it, then I'm leaving it there and trusting God at His word.

Overall, this experience really afforded me the privilege of knowing how awesome our God really is. For this, I will praise

Him and will not stop praising Him for who He is and what He has done through my life. My fervent prayer is that this book gives all that read it the same opportunity of knowing how powerful our God really is as well. Lift up your heads and know that our God is alive and He reigns for evermore!

James "Jay" Dewees

Introduction

On December 2, 2011, my life changed forever!

My husband, James (Jay), went to a wedding rehearsal where he had a forceful arrhythmia (heart gets out of rhythm) and collapsed--went into sudden cardiac arrest/death. This was not a heart attack, but a condition that can't be predicted or always explained. As a matter of fact, James was just given a clean bill of heart health by his doctors last month.

As God would have it, qualified nurses, CPR certified people, and prayer warriors were a part of His plan. When Jay collapsed, prayer was immediately offered and CPR was performed by several who were on hand for the wedding rehearsal until EMS got on the scene. Upon their arrival, the paramedics took over, using the defibrillators several times trying to bring Jay back. Had it not been for my assigned angel, Tarsha, the paramedics were ready to call it—yes, pronounce him dead. The outlook was so grim; several left the wedding rehearsal to spread the word that James L. Dewees was dead. Yes, according to all medical standards, he was gone, but God said, "Not now." He had to use this vessel to get Glory and remind everyone connected to him that He is in control! I am told that Jay was unconscious/flat lined for at least 40 minutes before his heart started beating on its own. A scientific wonder and miracle had taken place!

◄ DAY ONE ►

Friday, December 2

This Friday started out just like every other busy Friday in the Dewees' home. Jay left for work around 6 a.m. Before leaving, he kissed me on the cheek and said, "Goodbye." I said to myself why is he saying 'Goodbye'? It sounds so final. He usually says 'see ya later', 'so long', or 'have a good day'.

I dropped Justin off at school and headed to work. Justin and I say a prayer every morning in the drop off line. The prayer is so routine... I almost say it without thinking about the words. We always end with "and God, bring our family back together again safely this evening... in Jesus' name." Justin finishes off with an "Amen"! Little did I know that prayer would be the first request God needed for this miracle to occur.

I was scheduled to be in Orlando Saturday through Tuesday. I headed home early from work for a hair appointment and to shop for my mother-in-law, Rosetta, who was just transferred to Hallmark Rehabilitation Center after an extended illness. I spoke to my husband several times that day and all appeared well. He seemed rushed, but he had been very busy. I left the hair appointment around 2:30 p.m., shopped at Wal-Mart and headed over to see my mother-in-law. I spoke to Jay again from the rehab center and let him speak to his mother for a minute. We made an agreement that I would pick up Justin because he was still at work and would be in a hurry to make the 6 p.m. wedding rehearsal.

I ran more errands which put me back in my hometown of Summerville around 5:40 p.m.--just in time to wave at Jay as our cars passed. I am now convinced that God did not want Jay to physically interact with me or our son, Justin. He knew what had to happen and everything had to be on course and in place for this miracle. I remember being in Best Buy chasing this camera that went on sale. I even left there saying to myself, "What is wrong with you girl? You have plenty of time. Why are you set on wasting this time today?" Had I remained, I wouldn't have even had that slight encounter with my husband that afternoon.

Jay picked up the cell phone when he saw me turn onto Mallard Road heading home. We talked briefly and he headed to rehearsal. I told him to have a good time, and enjoy his old friends that came in for the wedding. I picked up Justin and settled in for the evening. I was scheduled to fly out the next morning to Orlando, but I wanted to finish decorating the Christmas tree and needed to finish packing. I noticed that our annual enrollment package wasn't done and today was the deadline. I sent Jay a text message asking for his work ID numbers and password to log on and complete our package. He texted me at 6:56 p.m. and called me with the password right after that. (I was told this was when he stepped out to get water before singing that last song at the rehearsal). He sounded really rushed and short of breath during the call, but I thought it had to do with the rehearsal.

I had some difficulty logging on and had to call for some technical assistance. During the call, I noticed Yakisha, my friend and church sister's, number on my caller ID. I didn't answer because I was so busy trying to finish the enrollment package. The doorbell rang while I was still on hold with technical support. It was Yakisha. She said, "Bridget, I need you". I immediately went into help mode – "Who? What? Where are your kids? I have some money. What do you need?" She handed me her cell phone and Tarsha explained that Jay had collapsed and that they were taking him to the hospital.

After the call ended, Yakisha said, "I am going to take you and Justin to Lady Jan's (First Lady of New Bethel Sounds of Praise Church) house and she is going to take you to meet them at the hospital. On second thought, I will keep Justin with me while you go to the hospital." I screamed, "Lady Jan can't drive me! She just had surgery herself!" However, God wanted that miracle lady to be by my side. Her experience was fresh and her faith was strong. As a matter of fact, God surrounded me with fresh miracles on that night. Yakisha had recently given birth to a 1 lb 1oz beautiful baby boy, who is amazingly healthy and strong now and Lady Jan had just come through brain surgery with miraculous results.

Lady Jan and Christian Simmons, our Executive Pastor, drove me to the hospital...the entire time knowing that Jay was not breathing, no heartbeat, and no pulse. God surrounded me with people who had crazy faith and could handle this situation with care. He strategically placed Tarsha, my church sister at the wedding rehearsal. Tarsha didn't even know the wedding party, but was asked to help out that night by the wedding director, Kim, who is also a church sister. Yakisha later told me that God strategically placed her only minutes from my house. Her children were already strapped in the car seats, and she was ready to roll as soon as she received the call from Tarsha. God was in control!

Lady Jan did all sorts of diversionary tactics, including pumping gas, to delay us getting to the hospital so that we would not arrive before the ambulance. Each time someone called her, she would say, "I have Bridget and we are on speaker phone". My heart was racing, but I had no idea of what was really going on. However, God said, "Trust me...I am not slack concerning my promises." I remember vividly the prayer we had in the car—I screamed, "God, please have mercy, just one more time!"

M   y   L   e   s   s   o   n
Always leave your loved ones in peace and harmony; you never know how you will see them the very next time.

The wedding party, including the bride and groom, my church family, parents and siblings, showed up at the hospital to pray for and support me. There were a host of people at the wedding rehearsal who witnessed the event. There were people from all denominations, friends, family, and members from my home church in Columbia who actually saw Jay collapse and die by all medical standards.

I was finally able to see Jay after a couple of hours. So, my 48-hour faith journey begins! There he lay looking like an angel. He had this unbelievable glow; so much so, the nurses kept asking me about his skin. I will never forget the conversation with the doctor. He was so calm, but painted a grim picture of facts about this type of recovery. Only 5-10% of folks come out of this, and the next 24-48 hours are crucial to his success. All I heard and knew was that Jay was coming out of this, whole and complete. My mind raced all over the place, but I knew it was time to be strong and stand on the Word.

Jay was taken to ICU and the hypothermia process to start cooling his body began. He had a special God fearing nurse assigned to him. I knew she was a believer and that God was giving her the directions needed to aid in his full recovery. Jay's body would just tremble as they continued to cool him down. He had a breathing tube, wires and IVs everywhere. The doctor even had to put a central line in his neck. My mom and dad got to the hospital that night from Columbia, and we stayed there until about 2:30 a.m. We all went home praying and me crying out to God. This was indeed the worst thing I have ever experienced in my entire life, but God gave me a peace that surpassed my own understanding.

Anyone who knows me, know I use Facebook to share with my family and friends updates and funny anecdotes throughout my day. God told me to share my events on Facebook just like I would share trips, Justin stories and everything else that was important to me.

FACEBOOK POSTS

Praying for my Jay.

◄ D A Y   T W O ►

S a t u r d a y ,   D e c e m b e r   3

None of us slept that night. I can truly say, I cried and prayed all night long. I headed out early with my mom to spend the day at the hospital. Lady Jan was right there with me. Tarsha brought me lunch. The short visits to ICU began. Loved ones, friends, church members, and family began to pour in. I spent more time in ICU to get rest than in the waiting room. I actually napped at the side of Jay's bed. I began to read scriptures and lay my hand on him to pray. Each time declaring a full recovery! I would say, "Jay, I am reading Psalm 27." I repeated.

☀ FACEBOOK POST

"Wait on the Lord, be of good courage and he shall strengthen thine Heart."

My mom is a pillar of strength and such a woman of faith. I remember saying, "Mom, they said Jay was out at least 40 minutes: no pulse, no heartbeat." Mom looked at me just as calm and collected and said, "And, Lazarus was out four days…what is forty minutes to God?" That statement erased all doubt from that moment on. Just as calmly, she turned back to her Bible and continued reading St. John 11.

M y L e s s o n
God is the same today, yesterday and forever. He is still in the miracle working business.

Several people poured in that morning and all day to pray with Jay. The bride's father, Pastor Grant, came in and just cried and prayed with us. I returned to the waiting area where my Mother was the entire time. She went in and prayed with Jay, as well. We were all sitting in the waiting room when the nurse came running out to get me. "Mrs. Dewees, he is awake; he is responding."

I rushed into the room to see Jay awake but incoherent. He still had all of the tubes and IVs everywhere. I could tell he was so scared and didn't have a clue what was going on. Also, he was heavily drugged. The nurse encouraged me to talk to him. It was then I realized that he recognized my voice and it was calming to him. I assured him that he would recover all. I told him what was going on. "Jay, you are cold on purpose, it is not your body. They have you cold so you can heal." He looked at me and tears rolled down the sides of his face. I would wipe his face, but he never saw me upset or crying. I was determined to be strong for Jay. God gave me so much strength in that room each time I visited my husband.

After a couple of minutes of talking to Jay, he would fall back to sleep. The nurses told me that they would be decreasing the meds over the next few hours to assess his progress. Each time Jay woke up, they would come running to get me. I would speak to him with the most positive voice and tone I had. "Jay, squeeze my hand." He did it. "Jay, where do you hurt … your chest?" He nods no. "Your throat?" He nods yes. "Jay you are going to be fine." He looks deep into my eyes. I will never forget that look, as if he was just hanging on to what I told him. In Genesis, God told Adam that he and Eve were no longer two, but one flesh. God allowed me to understand what that really meant as I interceded on my life partner's behalf. This part of the story was for my growth. I only cried behind Jay's back. I made sure that every visit was positive, and that people who entered the room had the right spirit. Yes, I was the police.

It was approaching 7 p.m., and Jay was warming nicely and showing great progress in blood pressure and heart rate. My friend, Debbie, who lived right down the street from the hospital, offered me a bed to take a nap. My family headed home and I was routed to Debbie's house for dinner and a nap. Of course, I hadn't packed a thing as who could be prepared for a situation like this? So, my friend went out and bought me a gown and toiletries. She demanded that I sleep. I set the alarm for 1 a.m. so I could get back on my post by my husband's side.

I learned during my time of rest, my husband had visitors which was terribly unfortunate as I'd told the nurse not to allow visitors in my absence. Remember, I'm the police. I had to shield my husband during this vulnerable time when he was at such a vulnerable state. Yes, I wanted to protect and cover my partner; he had to make it through this!

M   y   L   e   s   s   o   n
Visit only family members and very close friends in ICU--that is a very private place. Guard the door and ensure that only positive people enter the room.

◄DAY THREE►

Sunday, December 4

I woke up and was ready to go back to the hospital by 1:30 a.m. Debbie wouldn't let me go alone. She went with me and slept in the waiting room while I went in and out. I would sleep on the side of the bed rail, just watching Jay. As I mentioned earlier, Jay had such a glow on his face. He looked like he was 20 years old. I offered more prayer, and read more scriptures.

> **☀ FACEBOOK POST**
>
> I almost forgot how much I love my Jay, my one and only life partner for over 20 years. Thanking God for His grace and mercy. "Wait on the Lord, be of good courage and He shall strengthen thine HEART".

◄◄◄◄

I was totally out of myself and in another realm of worship… serving my husband. The nurses told me to go get some rest; they would be taking him off the breathing tube and heavy meds by noon on Sunday. I was confident that God had done this miracle and it was all about giving Him glory. I decided to go home, shower, change and steal a couple of hours of sleep, so I would be ready for the big events of the day. Debbie walked me to my car and I drove home. I fell in the bed, still tossing and turning.

I got up at 9 a.m., showered and was getting dressed when the phone rang – it was the hospital. For one second, a thousand things ran through my mind. I went numb. "Hello, Mrs. Dewees. We have a surprise for you." Seconds later, I hear my husband's voice. "Bridget, why am I in the hospital? What happened to me?" I actually lost it for a few seconds. I hollered

> **M y   L e s s o n**
>
> *Stay connected to righteous people, for their prayers availeth much. Guard your heart both naturally and spiritually. Store up your praises and prayers and God will redeem them in times of turmoil.*

out, "Mom, I am talking to Jay on the phone. Yes, he is talking, alert and wanting to know where he is!" We danced a while. Mom tried to take the phone out of my hand, but I had a grip and wouldn't let go. I let Jay know that I was on my way back to the hospital.

I wanted to run by New Bethel Sounds of Praise (NBSOP) and just run around the church. Instead, I called Lady Jan to give her the news. My First Lady just cried, cried, cried! I am told she went in the church, gave this praise report and church was out! I called my brother Ray, and he was overjoyed as well. Yes, a full miracle had taken place. Sunday service at so many of my friend's churches was just dedicated to giving God praise for this miracle.

FACEBOOK POST

I just had a two hour conversation with Jay, helped him stand up, he is talking and drinking! Miracle season. Can't stop praising God!!!

I was so excited! My sister, Sheila, drove me to the hospital. When we arrived, Sheila waited in the ICU waiting room and I ran in to see Jay who had 100 questions. I was giggling all over myself. I told him 10 times what happened, just a little bit at a time. I realized that he did not have memory of those events. I met with Dr. Ellerson who was just all smiles. He kept reminding me of how rare and uncommon this event was and for Jay to recover so well was just a miracle. He instructed me of our next steps and told me Jay would be just fine. God is GOOD!

We celebrated and danced around that hospital waiting room. I will never forget the maintenance staff lady who pushed her cart to the side and joined me in a praise dance in the waiting room. People all over that hospital heard about Jay and were giving God glory! My church family, friends, and family poured in to check on us all day long. Many came to see Jay sitting up and talking in ICU. What a glorious day!

FACEBOOK POST

Lord, I praise you.

I decided not to let our son, Justin, see his Dad unconscious in ICU. I just didn't want him to have that lasting picture in his little mind. We told him that Daddy was sick and that we must keep praying for him. Justin prayed for his daddy the entire weekend. Yakisha told me the heart wrenching story of Justin praying in the back seat that Friday night as she drove him to her house.

Jay asked about Justin from the time he woke up until he was finally able to see him. Jay's short term memory was a little "lazy" as the doctors explained it; so, he asked me the same questions over and over again. "Where is Justin?" I would explain that he was with Mom and Sheila. He would respond, "Oh, your mom is here? Sheila is here too?" I would confirm only to have him ask me the same questions 15 minutes later.

Justin was finally able to see his Daddy Sunday afternoon. I could tell he was nervous about being in the hospital room, but he put on his big boy face and said, "Hey, Daddy. What's up?" This is how they greet each other when they have been apart for a while. Amazing how the little things in life seem so big after an experience like this.

My family left the hospital with Justin late that afternoon. Although a somewhat shy little boy, my mom told me that Justin began to preach sermons and quote scriptures he heard over the years all the way home that night. He preached, "No weapon formed against us shall prosper! If the devil wanted to kill him, he should have done it in the night.... because *joy* is coming in the morning!"

I went home around 9 p.m. and was able to sleep a full 6 hours for the first time since this journey began.

◄DAY FOUR►

Monday, December 5

I got Justin off to school and headed out for the hospital, this time I had my overnight bag. I was determined to see Jay through the next few hours. We were moving to a regular room - Glory be to God! Out of ICU! God is good! Miracle!

The calls and visits were almost overwhelming. We are so loved and people just gave and gave of their time and resources. I saw cousins and friends I hadn't seen in years. Yes, they were coming to see this miracle. Each person left with a message of hope and an invitation to know God better! Jay and I were beginning to realize that this event was a responsibility given to us to proclaim God's healing power. It was all a setup for our next level.

The electrical heart doctors began to discuss the procedure of putting in a defibrillator. I didn't flinch or worry about this at all. God you brought us this far, you are going to take us on. We met with Dr. Frain and his assistant. I had to touch every doctor at least once; in my mind I was transferring God's glory and favor as they deal with Jay.

We settled in for the night: me on the visitor's recliner and Jay in his regular hospital room. The nurses came in and out all night. I must have told his testimony three times in my sleep.

◄DAY FIVE►

Tuesday, December 6

Today, we would be transferred to Roper Hospital for the defibrillator insertion. No worries at all. I was with Jay the entire time. My mom took care of Justin and the home. We went through it: just God, Jay and me. I didn't know which direction to take; so, I used social media to help me out.

Oh, boy! The word of God

lifted us all day long! I would read different scriptures to Jay throughout the day until the ambulance came for the transfer. I headed downtown in my car. The procedure was scheduled for 1 p.m. My pastor, Apostle Simmons, came down and prayed with us before the procedure. He told me, "I see what God is doing in you; I see your new strength." We met the doctors and

Jay headed into surgery. I had no worries. What is a little procedure after all we've come through this far?

The procedure was successful. I met Jay back at his room where he was to be on bed rest until 6 p.m. We had lunch, napped and just spent time together. Jay's co-worker and another church sister stopped by to share in the testimony. God is so good. I have absolutely no shame and even extra boldness about declaring the works of the Lord.

After 6 p.m., we took a short walk down the hall. This was Jay's first time walking since the event. Such a miracle! Every step he took was a 'thank you, Jesus' under my breath. Jay quickly realized that he had a little ways to go before full recovery. Nevertheless, the doctors told us he was going home tomorrow! What a journey!

☀ FACEBOOK POST
Praise report: I just took a walk with Jay down the hall. I was just told he can go home tomorrow!

What a mighty God we serve. We both decided that I should go home tonight and check on Justin and the house. Jay slept well and I slept an entire 8 hours.

M   y   L   e   s   s   o   n
Peace be still. God was in the boat the entire time.

FACEBOOK POST

It's all about Jesus! New day, new mercies.

I was scheduled to go on a school field trip with Justin and had to tell him that I had a bigger field trip today. Daddy was coming home! Justin decided that Daddy's coming home was more important and he went with me instead of the school trip.

▶▶▶▶

FACEBOOK POST

Lawd, I danced around the bed a while, got discharge papers!!!!!!

We headed downtown early with excitement! When we got to the hospital, Jay was awake and getting ready for breakfast. After a few more tests, and paper work, we were released. I think I was just numb by this time.

We got Jay dressed and ready to go. We loaded him in the car still sharing the testimony with strangers on the way out. I testified to the new nurses, the wheel chair attendant and anybody who would listen. My miracle was going home. Jay's mood was quiet and a little nervous, I was sure. We just wanted to keep him up and happy. Don't think about what happened to you; think about what is going to happen to your future.

We approached the neighborhood and drove into the garage. My mom was downstairs on the couch just waiting. Jay got out of the car and started his walk into his home. He said, "Well, Mother Pinckney, I made it home". Then he broke down. The three of us just embraced each other and cried for a few minutes. We assured Jay that he was going to be fine and all is well. What an emotional moment. I can only imagine what Jay was thinking. He couldn't talk much.

☀ FACEBOOK POST
Bridget is one happy house wife in da kitchen tonight cooking a heart healthy meal for my man.

Yes, we made it home with a testimony, a second chance at life, a clean slate, a chance to set real priorities, and we shall live to declare the works of the Lord! I love God and my family more than ever!

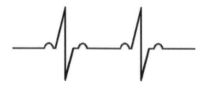

It has been two weeks and Jay is recuperating nicely! We are just in awe of God's love and mercy towards us. We are excited that God used Jay for such a time like this--to declare his amazing works during this Christmas season, not only us, but 65 people from the wedding party will spread this message that God is still performing miracles in this day! The doctors continue to reference Jay as a miracle. The cardiologist explained that he is a special case study, not fitting the textbook rules or predictions.

I am so in love with my brand new "miracle man"—God gave us a second chance to embrace life and each other. We don't know where Jay was those 40 minutes, but I am sure he will sing, play that saxophone and preach like never before. We are ready to declare the goodness of God wherever He takes us!

M y   L   e   s   s   o   n
Sometimes as strong, outgoing, professional women, we forget that God created us for the man. It is an honor to serve a Godly man. It was my pleasure and delight to serve my husband in this capacity. I am better, stronger and wiser for it.

FACEBOOK POST

Tonight, my family of three prayed together one more time. Justin thanked God for bringing Daddy home. I prayed for guidance and wisdom and Jay just thanked God he found him worthy to be used in this miraculous way-all for His Glory. Please keep praying for us—I love you all so much.

Reflections

► O N E ◄

Not Just Another Dream

God's ways are so far above our

thoughts. He is always in control and strategically prepares those He loves for the perfect storms that will come in our lives.

I was reminded of a dream I had about a month before all of this happened. I am not a dreamer so whenever I have one that lingers, I try to understand it. This one was a total nightmare. It was the craziest, scariest dream I ever remember having. It bothered me so much; I sat straight up in the bed and told it to Jay. I called my brother 6 a. m. on his way to work that morning. It really shook me up. Both Jay and my brother said that it was only a nightmare and brushed it off.

In the dream, I was diagnosed with a disease that usually leads to death. People had already written me off and were treating me as if I was dead already. I constantly repeated,

"What are you doing? I am not dead." I saw myself at a big ceremony and I couldn't figure it out. There were plenty of church folks and my doctor, but it wasn't a church service. All of my friends and family said goodbye to me alive and turned me over to the doctor who was acting as the embalmer. The doctor started with medicines that were supposed to start the process, but I would never die. Eventually, I was ushered down the aisle of a church with a white gown on. I was laid on a cooling board and my doctor said, I am going to have to use the vein in your neck to start the embalming process...I woke up!

I didn't get peace over this dream until I started to declare and proclaim the word of God. I said to myself over and over, I shall live and not die, with long life He shall satisfy me. I quoted every life scripture I knew. I finally was able to let the dream go.

The night of December 2nd, the doctor came out to the waiting room and asked me to sign a consent form. She said, "James is so weak, we can't get another IV in his arm. So, I need to use a central line in his neck." "A vein in his neck?" I said. At that moment, the dream came back to me. Everything in my dream related to this event! The ceremony was the wedding rehearsal or the actual wedding. A white dress is what a bride normally wears. Jay's sudden cardiac death directly related to my "demise" in the dream. Even the cooling board represented the cooling strips they laid Jay on to preserve his organs and cells.

The dream was not a prediction of what would happen, but it served to remind me that God had this planned the entire time and He was in full control! God gave me unbelievable strength from that point on. I was able to serve Jay and speak life and recovery over him. I dare not take any credit for this. If it were not for the prayers of the righteous and the multitude getting on one accord, my story would have ended much differently. All of this was and will forever be for the Glory of God!

► T W O ◄
Operating in the Gifts of the Spirit

I believe in the gifts of the spirit according to (I Corinthians 12:8-11) and I believe that they should be operating in the church. The Lord used two people, in particular, to prepare me for this perfect storm.

Toward the end of last year (2010), we were having one of those typical New Bethel Sounds of Praise services where gifts were operating in the church. An Elder walked over to me, kneeled down beside me, took my right hand and placed it in his. He told me, "God said, 'Your husband's healing is in your hands.'" I just looked at him trying to understand what he meant. At that time, I thought it meant that I was to cook the right foods and manage the house in a way that would keep him healthy. Those words came back to me a year later as I stood in ICU.

Last summer, a woman visited our church passing through the town. I had never seen her before and she didn't know one thing about me or my husband. After service, I greeted her and thanked her for coming—just being cordial. She began to tell me that God has a book for me to write. She said that the book will be about you and your husband's journey and it will bless this nation. Honestly, I can't even remember her name or even what she looks like, but that prophecy never left me.

Jay and I have been married for 21 years. I thought to my-self, yes, there are several things I could write about concerning our journey. Each time I would start to write, I would get writer's block. I could never finish a story; however, I sat down and organized this little book in just two days. This was the book she told me about! I had no idea God was going to use us in this way! Each time we share the story, we look at each other like this can't be true and we are just humbled by God's mercy and favor over our lives.

These are the last days my friends, I encourage each of you to find yourselves in a place where you are free to use the gifts that God has given you. He gave us these gifts to be a blessing to the kingdom and I believe we live so far beneath our privileges when the gifts are not being used freely.

▶ T H R E E ◀

A Special Visitation for Confirmation

> **☀ FACEBOOK POST - Tarsha**
> I had a wonderful time with my miracle family tonight.

My assigned angel, Tarsha, and her husband came by to visit Jay and me at our home. This was the first conversation Jay and I had with Tarsha together; so, Jay asked her to give him all of the details about this event including her role and a play by play of what happened. Remember, Jay's short term memory was completely wiped out for that entire weekend.

Tarsha began to tell us that Jay had just sung his second song. He sang *"Jesus, you are the center of my Joy"* first, then the selection for the bridal march. She explained that Jay calmly sat down in the chair—with both hands up and he just kept leaning back in the chair. The people around him immediately noticed that something was wrong, and the registered nurses, who just happened to be in the wedding party, immediately went to work on Jay. Tarsha said one nurse yelled, "We don't have a pulse." At that moment, she called 911. The nurses and CPR trained worked on Jay until EMS arrived.

Tarsha described the atmosphere in the church as being very calm. Many were praying on their knees and in chairs. Jay was sitting on the platform. Everyone could see him. The situation was so scary; all children were removed from the sanctuary. She said that Jay turned black and blue and his stomach had swollen like a pregnant woman. He was lifeless. The nurses would switch off doing CPR, but they were getting exhausted. Finally, EMS got there and began to work on him.

During this time, Tarsha had my assigned angel, Yakisha, on the phone and was telling her the situation. Yakisha never let on to me that this was going on. The paramedics asked Tarsha to ask me if Jay had a Do Not Resuscitate (DNR) order. She admonished the paramedics to keep working! She exclaimed, "He has a nine year old and a wife and I am not going to ask her that!"

Jay was rolled out of the church on a gurney with his legs dangling lifelessly as EMS continued working on him. Tarsha followed the gurney out of the church, but not before she turned around waving her hands demanding, "Everyone, keep praying!

Jay is going to live and not die! He shall declare the works of the Lord".

Tarsha explained that she tailed EMS all the way to the hospital. She prayed, prayed and prayed all the way. She told us that the highway where EMS had to pull out is known for excessive traffic. However, that Friday night, there wasn't a car in sight! Tarsha said that she saw the paramedics working on Jay the entire ride to the hospital. It wasn't until they made the turn into the hospital parking lot, that Jay's heart started beating again.

My husband was just floored to hear Tarsha's story. He said if there weren't so many witnesses, he wouldn't believe it himself. We met Tarsha after joining New Bethel in 2007. Tarsha is one of the sweetest, soft spoken, young ladies I have ever met. She is a powerful prayer warrior with crazy faith. She and her husband have several miracle stories of their own. Tarsha started referring to me as her mentor a few months ago, but now she is my mentor and forever prayer partner. I am so grateful that she listened to the voice of God and kept the faith.

Tarsha's crazy faith reminded me that our God is the same God that raised Lazarus from the dead. God has given us a 21st century Lazarus experience all for His glory! Now that you know God is still a miracle working God, claim yours! By your faith, He will and can make you whole. He is a healer, a deliverer, a way maker, and can do anything but fail.

Excerpts from St. John 11

3-5

Therefore his sisters sent unto him, saying, Lord, behold, he whom thou lovest is sick. When Jesus heard that, he said, This sickness is not unto death, but for the glory of God, that the Son of God might be glorified thereby. Now Jesus loved Martha, and her sister, and Lazarus.

23

Jesus saith unto her, Thy brother shall rise again.

40

Jesus saith unto her, Said I not unto thee, that, if thou wouldest believe, thou shouldest see the glory of God?

43-44

And when he thus had spoken, he cried with a loud voice, Lazarus, come forth. And he that was dead came forth, bound hand and foot with graveclothes: and his face was bound about with a napkin. Jesus saith unto them, Loose him, and let him go.

A Light for the Journey

Lord, thy Word was indeed a lamp unto my feet and a light unto my path.
Psalm 119:105

Below are the scriptures sent to me from friends and family during this testing time:

2 Timothy 1:7

For God hath not given us the spirit of fear; but of power, and of love, and of a sound *mind.*

Acts 2: 1-4

And when the day of Pentecost was fully come, they were all with one accord in one place. And suddenly there came a sound from heaven as of a rushing mighty wind, and it filled all the house where they were sitting. And there appeared unto them cloven tongues like as of fire, and it sat upon each of them. And they were all filled with the Holy Ghost, and began to speak with other tongues, as the Spirit gave them utterance

Ephesians 3:20

Now unto him that is able to do exceeding abundantly above all that we ask or think, according to the power that worketh in us.

Ephesians 6:10-11

Finally, my brethren, be strong in the Lord, and in the power of his might. Put on the whole armor of God, that ye may be able to stand against the wiles of the devil.

Galatians 2:20

I am crucified with Christ: nevertheless I live; yet not I, but Christ liveth in me: and the life which I now live in the flesh I live by the faith of the Son of God, who loved me, and gave himself for me.

Hebrews 11:6

But without faith it is impossible to please him: for he that cometh to God must believe that he is, and that he is a rewarder of them that diligently seek him.

I Corinthians 13:7-8

Beareth all things, believeth all things, hopeth all things, endureth all things. Charity never faileth: but whether there be prophecies, they shall fail; [1] whether there be tongues, they shall cease; whether there be knowledge, it shall vanish away.

Isaiah 40:4-5

Every valley shall be exalted, and every mountain and hill shall be made low: and the crooked shall be made straight, and the rough places plain: And the glory of the Lord shall be revealed, and all flesh shall see it together: for the mouth of the Lord hath spoken it.

Isaiah 53:1-5

Who hath believed our report and to whom is the arm of the Lord revealed? For he shall grow up before him as a tender plant, and as a root out of a dry ground: he hath no form nor comeliness; and when we shall see him, there is no beauty that we should desire him. He is despised and rejected of men; a man of sorrows, and acquainted with grief: and we hid as it were our faces from him; he was despised, and we esteemed him not. Surely he hath borne our griefs, and carried our sorrows: yet we did esteem him stricken, smitten of God, and afflicted. But he was wounded for our transgressions, he was bruised for our iniquities: the chastisement of our peace was upon him; and with his stripes we are healed.

Isaiah 54:17

No weapon that is formed against thee shall prosper; and every tongue that shall rise against thee in judgment thou shalt condemn. This is the heritage of the servants of the Lord, and their righteousness is of me, saith the Lord.

Jeremiah 17:14

Heal me, O Lord, and I shall be healed; save me, and I shall be saved: for thou art my praise.

Jeremiah 29:11

For I know the thoughts that I think toward you, saith the Lord, thoughts of peace, and not of evil, to give you an expected end.

Mark 11:22-24

And Jesus answering saith unto them, Have faith in God. For verily I say unto you, That whosoever shall say unto this mountain, Be thou removed, and be thou cast into the sea; and shall not doubt in his heart, but shall believe that those things which he saith shall come to pass; he shall have whatsoever he saith. Therefore I say unto you, What things soever ye desire, when ye pray, believe that ye receive them, and ye shall have them.

Matthew 6:33

But seek ye first the kingdom of God, and his righteousness; and all these things shall be added unto you.

Philippians 3:14

I press toward the mark for the prize of the high calling of God in Christ Jesus.

Philippians 4:7-8

And the peace of God, which passeth all understanding, shall keep your hearts and minds through Christ Jesus. Finally, brethren, whatsoever things are true, whatsoever things are honest, whatsoever things are just, whatsoever things are pure, whatsoever things are lovely, whatsoever things are of good report; if there be any virtue, and if there be any praise, think on these things.

Psalm 1:3

And he shall be like a tree planted by the rivers of water, that bringeth forth his fruit in his season; his leaf also shall not wither; and whatsoever he doeth shall prosper.

Psalm 111:1-3

Praise ye the Lord. I will praise the Lord with my whole heart, in the assembly of the upright, and in the congregation. 2 The works of the Lord are great, sought out of all them that have pleasure therein. 3 His work is honourable and glorious: and his righteousness endureth for ever.

Psalm 121:1

I will lift up mine eyes unto the hills, from whence cometh my help.

Psalm 124:1

If it had not been the Lord who was on our side…

Psalm 8:1

O Lord our Lord, how excellent is thy name in all the earth! who hast set thy glory above the heavens.

Psalm 27:14

Wait on the Lord: be of good courage, and he shall strengthen thine heart: wait I say, on the Lord.

Psalm 91:14-16

Because he hath set his love upon me, therefore will I deliver him: I will set him on high, because he hath known my name. He shall call upon me, and I will answer him: I will be with him in trouble; I will deliver him, and honour him. With long life will I satisfy him, and shew him my salvation.

Psalm 34:17-19

The righteous cry, and the LORD heareth, and delivereth them out of all their troubles. The LORD is nigh unto them that are of a broken heart; and saveth such as be of a contrite spirit. Many are the afflictions of the righteous: but the LORD delivereth him out of them all.

Psalm 37:23-24

The steps of a good man are ordered by the Lord: and he delighteth in his way. Though he fall, he shall not be utterly cast down: for the Lord upholdeth him with his hand.

Romans 12:1-2

I beseech you therefore, brethren, by the mercies of God, that ye present your bodies a living sacrifice, holy, acceptable unto God, which is your reasonable service. 2 And be not conformed to this world: but be ye transformed by the renewing of your mind, that ye may prove what is that good, and acceptable, and perfect, will of God.

Romans 8:28

And we know that all things work together for good to them that love God, to them who are the called according to his purpose.

Facebook Posts from Friends

Friends' Posts of Encouragement and Thanksgiving

☀ FACEBOOK POST

I read, with awe, your testimony. I only had one question, when you stated that you didn't know where you found the strength. My dear, sweet, ray of absolute sunshine friend, like Dorothy in the Wizard of Oz, you had it all along. You are a Steele magnolia in thought, word, deed and action. When you heard Jay had a five to ten percent chance of coming through, that is what you heard, that he would recover, while others might have withered and asked God, why? You merely, put Jay's recovery on path and didn't even consider an alternative. You prayed, you stated that there would be a full recovery and set the path in motion never wavering. You are a vital part of Jay's recovery. You need not question your strength; I never have my dear friend.

☀ FACEBOOK POST

I visit your Facebook page every chance I get because it encourages me. I was present that night, and my mind raced all night, but I know we truly serve a GREAT GOD!! I get JOY every time I read your post. Be strong and I will continue to keep your family in my prayers. Be Blessed ☺

FACEBOOK POST

Praying for my brother Jay. You have already overcome. Just a test for the awesome testimony that Jay will deliver. God is preparing Jay to go to another level in Him. Eyes have not seen, neither have your ears heard what the Dewees family is getting ready for. Increase and promotion to another level. Love you guys much, and I have such admiration for the anointing on your life. Girl, get ready. It is your time and season to go into another realm in God........ Marvelous works in store....

 FACEBOOK POST

I'm going to have to start calling you the woman at the well. The woman was the perfect tool needed to go spread the word about who He is. No mystery as to why he chose your family. You are the vessel he is using to spread the gospel to a dying world. He has you and your family in his plan. I'm just glad to know you. love you sis.

 FACEBOOK POST

Bridget, you are just what God has ordained for such a time as this. All the word that you have stored in your heart thru your mouth, ears and eyes was waiting just for this time. God knew that it was there and now it was time for Bridget to let it out of her mouth. Keep that mouth full of the Word girl. We are still praying and believing God for even greater manifestation of himself. I love you my daughter, continue to stay connected. To God be the glory!!!!!!!!!

☀ FACEBOOK POST

I don't have the words to express my joy and excitement! To God be the glory for the things He has done. I've been sharing this testimony all week long and will continue to do so. You have set such a wonderful example for me and other women and this story just put the icing on the cake. You are the ultimate example of grace under fire. I'm so grateful for what God has done for you and Jay (and Justin) and honored that the Lord saw fit to allow our paths to cross. I love you Sis!!!!

☀ FACEBOOK POST

Wow, Bridget, you and Jay are truly blessed! My eyes fill with tears every time I see a new update from you. I'm so glad for a miraculous report and not a sad one! To God be the glory and thank you both for being a lesson for us all! I will NOT take life for granted - mine or that of the ones I love! I love you, sis!!!

☀ FACEBOOK POST

Bridget what an AWESOME story. I'm so glad that you posted this. I shared Jay's story with some co-workers, but did not have the entire story...now I do and will read this to my co-workers on Monday. Tears of joy, tears of thanksgiving for you and your family! "God is still in con-trol!"

☀ FACEBOOK POST

I'm in tears....tears of joy. Just know how awesome our God is. I cried out to God for Jay, you and Justin. It is my continued prayer that God wraps his loving arms around your entire family. This is indeed a Christmas miracle. I will share your family's testimony with my family and church family. We are connected in the spirit. I have Jay's cd packed in my bag that I will carry with me to the hospital and will listen while in labor. Thank you for sharing this awesome testimony.

☀ FACEBOOK POST

Praise the Lord! I heard about Jay while I was in Africa and we put him before the throne of God literally from the other side of the world. Let me know how things are going. I am driving home now from Atlanta. God bless!

☀ FACEBOOK POST

What a mighty God we serve! God used this to let our family know that God is still God and that He is still a healer! Love you Guys!!

☀ FACEBOOK POST

God is an awesome God. I praise Him for showing up and proving that miracles can still happen in these days and times.

FACEBOOK POST

It was soooo good hearing Jay's voice last night. Now, I truly under-stand what Martha and Mary felt regarding their brother. Knowing scientifically this is not possible but to see God work the impossible... Oh my GOD... HE has given me so much hope and not just myself but to all of the believers. For Jay is... A LIVING TESTIMONY.. Love you all.. #stillpraying

FACEBOOK POST

Bridget, this is a life changing miracle not only for you and Jay but for so many that witness it and for those that will hear about it, I'm sharing it with anyone that will listen! Our God is an awesome God!! So very happy for you and your family!

FACEBOOK POST

Thank you for keeping us posted on God's goodness, mercy and miracles...You are sharing the gospel through your messages. Thank God that your husband is doing well! GOD continues to do marvelous things...Praise the LORD!

FACEBOOK POST

Wow, Bridget...I logged on this morning and saw your statuses about Jay; so glad to know he is doing well!!! I went to a live Christmas drama last night titled "This Man Called Jesus", and a really emotional part was concerning the many miracles that were done when Jesus walked the earth. It is so good to know the miracles DID NOT CEASE, because of the authority that was given to us IN JESUS NAME!! Love ya!

FACEBOOK POST

The fervent effectual Prayer of the righteous availeth much!!!! Many of God's people are praying and interceding for Healing, Restoration, Peace and The abundant power that will come out of this testimony. Many will now know that God is still working miracles of Healing and issuing strength to go through what seems to be the impossible. I Love you both and am here for you.

The Dewees Family

**Ordinary People Chosen
for an Extraordinary
Experience**

About the Author

 **_Bridget P. Dewees_** is an award winning Quality Practitioner with more than 20 years of professional experience in Business, Finance, Teaching and Higher Education Administration. Bridget is a South Carolina Champion for Excellence award recipient, presented by the SC Quality Forum to a South Carolina resident who is widely recognized within their organization as being able to ignite desires in others for the unending quest for quality.

Bridget's first love is Jesus Christ. She accepted Christ at the young age of twelve years old. Since that time, she has served in various roles in church administration including, Sunday School Superintendent, Youth Ministry, and Young Women's Auxiliaries. She is currently a member of the New Bethel Sounds of Praise Pentecostal Fellowship Ministries in Summerville, SC. She is married to her best friend, James; and they have one son, Justin.

Bridget has a Master's degree in Business Administration from Webster University and a Bachelor of Science degree in Accounting from the University of South Carolina. She is currently a candidate for a PhD in Management, Leadership and Organizational Change at Walden University.

Contact James and Bridget:
21st Century Lazarus Experience Ministry
lazarus21experience@yahoo.com

Made in the USA
Columbia, SC
08 July 2021